# 14 Days of Spiritual Recharge

## Tasha M. Crafton

14 Days of Spiritual Recharge

Published by Semaj Publishing

ISBN: 978-0-9981103-8-7

# Table of Contents

# *Introduction*

I want to take this moment to remind you that you are victorious because of your faith and obedience unto God as you embark on a 14-day journey of fasting, praying, declaring and recharging. If you have been struggling with challenges that appear to be a cycle of issues, this book is for you; this fast is for you! If your life has been stagnant and you feel like you are constantly walking in place, but not growing, this book is for you, this fast is for you! If you are facing challenges with your health or relationships, this book is for you, this fast is for you!

Prayer combined with fasting gives you divine access to God, an advantage over the enemy and puts you in proper relationship with God.   God, prayer, and fasting produce great spiritual results.

The book of Matthew declares how we must present ourselves during a fast.

Matthew 6:16-18:

> *16 "When you fast, do not look somber as the hypocrites do, for they disfigure their faces to show others they are fasting. Truly I tell you, they have received their reward in full.*

> *17 But when you fast, put oil on your head and wash your face,*

> *18 so that it will not be obvious to others that you are fasting, but only your Father, who unseen; and your Father, who sees what is done in secret will reward you.*

# *Day 1*

Psalm 51:1-13 expresses one of the clearest examples of repentance in all scriptures. Countless broken sinners have found in these words an exquisite expression of their deeply felt need for God's mercy and forgiveness. David's confession has helped people examine excuses, half-hearted repentance, and lack of sorrow over sin that can keep them from experiencing pardon. David's words also demonstrate the place of hope within confession. Use this Psalm as a starting point when dealing with a sense of distance or with guilt that is affecting your relationship with God. It will help you identify and rectify sin in your life through confession and repentance.

Psalm 51:1-13:

> *¹Have mercy upon me, O God, according to your unfailing love; according to your great compassion blot out my transgressions.*
>
> *²Wash away all my iniquity and cleanse me from my sin.*
>
> *³ For I know my transgressions and my sins is always before me.*
>
> *⁴ Against you, you only, have I sinned and done what is evil in your sight; so you are right in your verdict and justified when you judge.*
>
> *⁵ Surely I was sinful at birth, sinful from the time my mother conceived me.*

*6Yet you desired faithfulness even in the womb; you taught me wisdom in that secret place.*

*7Cleanse me with hyssop, and I will be clean; wash me, and I will be whiter than snow.*

*8Let me hear joy and gladness; let the bones you have crushed rejoice.*

*9Hide your face from my sins and blot out all my iniquity.*

*10Create in me a pure heart, O God, and renew a steadfast spirit within me.*

*11Do not cast me from your presence or take your Holy Spirit from me.*

*12Restore to me the joy of your salvation and grant me a willing spirit, to sustain me.*

*13Then I will teach transgressors your ways, so that sinners will turn back to you.*

In Psalm 51:1-7 David was truly sorry for his adultery with Bathsheba and for murdering her husband to cover it up. He knew that his actions hurt many people. But because David repented of those sins, God mercifully forgave him. No sin is too great to be forgiven!

Do you feel that you could never come close to God because you have done something terrible? God can and will forgive you for any sin. While God forgives us, He does not always erase the natural consequences of our sin. David's life and family were never the same as a result of what he had done.

Psalms 51:4 says that although David had sinned with Bathsheba, David said that he had sinned against God. When someone steals, murders, or slanders, it is against someone else - a victim. According to the world's standards, extramarital sex between two consenting adults is acceptable if nobody gets hurt. But people do get hurt in David's case; a man was murdered, and a baby died. All sin hurts us and others, but ultimately it offends God because sin in any form is rebellion against God's way of living. When you are tempted to do wrong, remember that you will be sinning against God. This may help you avoid danger.

Let's look at Psalms 51:5, 7 and 10: Because we were born sinners our natural inclination is to please ourselves rather than God. *(51:5)* David followed that inclination when he took another man's wife. Like David, we must ask God to cleanse us from within filling our hearts and spirits with new thoughts and desires. *(51:7)* Right conduct can come only from a clean heart and spirit. Ask God to create a pure heart and spirit within you. *(51:10)*

Do you ever feel stagnant in your faith, as though you are just going through the motions? Has sin ever driven a wedge between you and God, making Him seem distant? David felt this way. He sinned with Bathsheba and had just been confronted by Nathan the prophet. In his prayer he cried, "Restore to me the joy of Your salvation". *(Psalm 51:12)* God wants us to be close to Him and to receive His full and complete life. But sin that remains unconfessed makes such intimacy impossible. Confess your sins to God. You may still have to face some earthly consequences, as David did, but God will give back the joy of your relationship with Him.

1 Corinthians 9:27 says:

> *[27]No, I strike a blow to my body and make it my slave so that after I have preached to others, I myself will not be disqualified for the prize.*

When Paul says he might be disqualified, he does not mean that he could lose his salvation, but rather that he could lose his privilege of telling others about Christ. It is easy to tell others how to live than to take our own advice. We must be careful to practice what we preach!

The bible also gives us divine instructions through Jesus Christ on the steps we must take to break every demonic stronghold in our lives.

Mark 9:29 says:

> *[29]He replied, "This kind can come out only by prayer."*

The disciples would often face difficult situations that could only be resolved through prayer. Prayer is the key that unlocks faith in our lives. Effective prayer needs both the attitude of complete dependence and the action of asking. Prayer demonstrates our reliance on God as we humbly invite Him to fill us with faith and power. There is no substitute for prayer, especially in circumstances that seem impossible.

### *Declarations:*

Father in Jesus' name, I decree and declare by the supreme authority of the Almighty God, that any hidden agenda of the enemy to create fear and frustration within myself or others will be blocked and destroy. May the sword of the Lord be my shield on today.

I decree and declare that I will not forfeit my destiny, but I shall receive the blessings of the Lord in this season! Now, I declare that I am a Winner!!! In Jesus' name, Amen!

# *Day 2*

Well, you made it through the first day by God's grace! As we enter into the second day of a winning season, I want you to know that you will finish strong, and you will begin to see the manifestations of victories!

The bible declares in the book of Jeremiah 29:11:

> *[11]For I know the plans I have for you," declares the LORD, "plans to prosper you and not to harm you, plans to give you hope and a future.*

We're all encouraged by a leader who stirs us to move ahead, someone who believes we can do the task that they have given and who will be with us all the way. God is that kind of leader. He knows the future, and His plans for us are good and full of hope. As long as God provides our agenda and goes with us as we fulfill His mission, we can have boundless hope. This does not mean that we will be spared pain, suffering, or hardship, but that God will see us through to a glorious conclusion.

Beloved, God has great plans for you and you must believe beyond what you see, feel or hear! Believe that you are getting ready to experience a release in your mind; renewed mindset, renewed spirit, and renewed strength. God is going to do a supernatural release in your finances, marriage, job, health and your family. God is releasing clarity and vision upon you like never before! You will be able to discern what is of God and what is of the enemy.

The Word declares in Matthew 21:22,

> *22If you believe, you will receive whatever you ask for in prayer."*

and Mark 11:24 says,

> *24Therefore I tell you, whatever you ask for in prayer, believe that you have received it, and it will be yours.*

So, don't give up on your dreams or visions that God has given you and placed in your belly; the business, books, non-profit organizations, boutique, hair salon, returning to school, starting your ministry, new home or new car. Whatever you're seeking and believing God for, believe that in this season, you will see the manifestation of every dream and vision come to pass.

## *Declarations:*
Father in Jesus' name, I decree and declare Matthew 21:22 and Mark 11:24 over my life. You said if you believe you will receive whatever you ask in prayer and you also said, whatever things you ask when you pray, believe that you receive them, and you will have them. I believe that you will renew my mind, spirit, and strength. I believe that you will release Ephesians 3:20 over my life, you will do exceedingly abundantly above all I ask, think and even imagine in my finances, ministry, education, health, and my family life. I decree and declare as of today I will not miss the timing of God's release due to procrastination, laziness, impatience, and disobedience. I decree and declare that every financial drought will dry up and wither away and lack is no longer my portion. God, you said, you would withhold no good thing from me. I decree and declare that you will not withhold your favor from my life and everyone that is connected to me. In Jesus' name, Amen!

# *Day 3*

Welcome to day 3, I pray that you're encouraged thus far The enemy's job is to kill, steal and destroy and his goal is to keep you in bondage. But, I want to remind you that the joy of the Lord is your strength. We are instructed to cast our cares on God because He cares for us. So, whatever is keeping you bound, stealing your joy, peace and rest, I encourage you to write down three things that seem to be taking your focus, robbing you of your peace and pushing you out of a relationship with God.

Matthew 11:28-30 states:

> *28 "Come to me, all you who are weary and burdened, and I will give you rest.*
>
> *29 Take my yoke upon you and learn from me, for I am gentle and humble in heart, and you will find rest for your souls.*
>
> *30 For my yoke is easy and my burden is light."*

A yoke is a heavy wooden harness that fits over the shoulders of an ox or oxen. It is attached to a piece of equipment the oxen are to pull. A person may be carrying heavy burdens of:

1. Sin
2. Excessive demands of religious leaders
3. Oppression and persecution
4. Weariness in the search for God

Jesus frees people from all these burdens. The "rest" that Jesus promises is love, healing, and peace with God, not the end of all labor. A relationship with God changes meaningless, wearisome toil into spiritual productivity and purpose.

In verse 30, in what sense was Jesus' yoke easy? The yoke emphasizes the challenges, work, and difficulties of partnering with Christ in life. Responsibilities weigh us down, even the effort of staying true to God. But Jesus' yoke remains easy compared to the crushing alternative. Jesus doesn't offer a life of luxurious ease; the yoke is still an oxen's tool for working hard. For us with God it's a shared yoke, with the weight falling on bigger shoulders than yours. Someone with more pulling power is upfront helping. Suddenly you are participating in life's responsibilities with a great Partner and now that frown can turn into a smile and that gripe into a song.

### *Declarations:*

Father in Jesus' name, I decree and declare by the power of the Holy Spirit, I am victorious, I am no longer a victim or will be victimized by the power of Darkness. I decree and declare that I will walk in the peace of God, the peace that surpasses all my understanding. God, You are not a God of disorder but of peace. You are the One who gives peace, not the world. I decree and declare authority over every demonic spirit that will try to suppress, oppress and cause me to be depressed. I decree and declare the same authority that Jesus has to trample over every serpent, scorpion, and demon of depression, oppression, insecurities, lack of confidence, and suicidal thoughts in Jesus' name. Isaiah 54:17 says, "No weapon formed against you shall prosper, And every tongue *which* rises against you in Judgement, you shall condemn." I am taking authority over my life; I surrender my old habits, ways, and thoughts to You. I take Your yoke upon my life because it is easy. I surrender my life to You so that I may rest in You. In Jesus' name, Amen!

# *Day 4*

I challenge you to take a stand against the enemy and push back on him and his tactics by commanding your peace today. Peace comes when you trust in God with all your heart.

As you pray today, ask God to secure your borders and double your protection, so that the enemy will not be able to penetrate your Spirit or your family.

Now, take this time to say to yourself, "I will trust God forever, and no good thing will be withheld from Me in Jesus' name."

Isaiah 26:3 declares:

> *3You will keep him in perfect peace those whose minds are steadfast, because they trust in you.*

### *Declarations:*
Father in Jesus' name, I decree and declare on this day that I will trust God beyond any circumstances, and I will have confidence in knowing that every obstacle that the enemy has sent to block me from moving forward has been destroyed by the authority and power of God. I decree and declare that everything that will try to infiltrate my mind with doubt, worry, insecurities, and anxiety that the Power of the Holy Spirit will overturn and arrest the assignment of the enemy, In Jesus' name, Amen!

# *Day 5*

Thank God you made it to day 5 of your spiritual recharge fast. As you may know the number 5 represents grace and I am grateful that God's grace is sufficient. Every day that you wake up is a new day of grace and mercies. It is a day that you have never seen before and the manifestation of God's grace upon your home, marriage, job, children, business, ministry and so much more. It is the saving grace that keeps the enemy from destroying, killing and stealing from you. The amazing thing about grace is that it is unmerited. It is not about works, but it is about God's grace that keeps us from hurt, harm, and danger.

So, today I challenge you in your prayer time to reflect on your life and all the times when God's grace has kept you. Meditate on God's goodness and mercy, and thank Him. Think about how many times we have taken God's grace for granted.

Pray, repent and thank Him. We have to be careful about how we handle His grace.

2 Corinthians 12:9 says:

> *9 But he said to me, "My grace is sufficient for you, for my power is made perfect in weakness." Therefore I will boast all the more gladly about my weaknesses, so that Christ's power may rest on me.*

In this verse, although God did not remove Paul's affliction, He promised to demonstrate His power in Paul.

The fact that God's power is displayed in our weaknesses should give us courage and hope. As we recognize our limitations, we will depend more on God for our effectiveness rather than on our energy, effort or talent. Our limitations not only help develop Christian character but also deepen our worship, because in admitting them we affirm God's strength.

### *Declarations:*

Father in Jesus' name, I decree and declare that today I will never take your grace for granted. I will be careful how I handle your grace upon my life, family, business, ministry, and job. God forgive me when I have taken You for granted. I decree and declare that every demonic spirit that would try to bring me out of a right relationship with You is exposed, revealed and my adversaries are made known and destroyed, dismantled and annihilated by the Power of the Holy Spirit. In Jesus' name, Amen!

# *Day 6*

Oh, give thanks to the Lord, for He is good. For His mercy endures forever. You made it to day 6 of your spiritual recharge fast.

God's Word is true and wonderful. Stay true to God and His Word no matter how bad the world becomes. Obedience to God's laws is the only way to achieve real happiness.

We are surrounded in a sea of sinful attractions, sexual images, gossip, malice, backbiting, slander, murder, incest, covetousness, unforgiveness, suicide, depression and much more. Everywhere we look or go we find temptation to fill our minds with impure thoughts, intent, and relationships that God does not approve. My question to you beloved, how do you stay pure in a contaminated environment? We cannot do this on our own but we must have counsel and strength more dynamic than the tempting influences around us. How can we find that strength and wisdom? The answer is by reading God's Word.

Hiding (keeping) God's Word in our hearts is a distraction and deterrent to sin. This alone should encourage you to meditate and memorize scripture. But, understand that memorizing scripture alone will not keep us from sin, you must also put God's Word to work.

You must wear God's Word around your neck like a necklace and keep God's Word on the tablet of your heart so you can overcome the temptations of your environment.

Psalms 119:9-11 says,

> *9How can a young person stay on the path of purity? By living according to your word.*

> *10I seek you with all my heart; do not let me stray from your commands.*

> *11I have hidden your word in my heart that I might not sin against you.*

God's Word is a revival kit; it revives dead areas in our lives. What you once thought was dead, God's Word can revive; your marriage, family, business, dreams, visions and even your ministry.

### *Declarations:*

Father in Jesus' name, I decree and declare that on day 6 of my spiritual recharge, I will meditate on your Word day and night. I will hide Your Word in my heart that I may not sin against it. I decree and declare that I will take heed to every word, precepts, and commandments, that I may be cleansed from every toxic relationship, soul tie, and stronghold. I decree and declare that your Word would be a lamp unto my feet. Out of the heart the mouth speaks, so I decree and declare that every demonic suggestion and activity will diminish by the Power of the Holy Spirit. I decree and declare that I will resist the devil and he will flee from my life. I decree and declare that I will not give in to the snare of entrapment of the enemy. In Jesus' name, Amen!

# *Day* 7

"He who has begun a good work in you will complete it until the day of Jesus Christ." Philippians 1:6

Praise the Lord beloved, you are at the halfway mark; day 7 of your spiritual recharge. The number 7 represents divine completion, perfection or the end of a thing.

Ecclesiastes 7:8 says,

> *7The end of a matter is better than its beginning, and patience is better than pride.*

In the beginning, you may have struggled to stay on the spiritual recharge fast; know that in the end you will reap the benefits, your Spirit will be recharged, refreshed, restored and your mind will be reset. By faith, whatever you need from God over the next seven days, through your prayers and declarations, it shall surely come to pass.

Beloved, God knows everything that you need. You are entering into a place of your needs being met. God said, in Philippians 4:19, "And my God will meet all your needs according to the riches of his glory in Christ Jesus."

As you walk with God and seek His face, you will have options in every area of your life. He will complete what He started in you.

I challenge you today to begin to examine yourself and the areas in your life that you need God to deliver you. Assess your surroundings, your friends and connections. Ask God for divine direction as to what needs to stay and what needs to go. Now, make a list and pray and declare over it for the next seven days believing God for the victory.

Philippians 1:4-6 says,

> *⁴ In all my prayers for all of you, I always pray with joy*
>
> *⁵ because of your partnership in the gospel from the first day until now,*
>
> *⁶ being confident of this, that he who began a good work in you will carry it on to completion until the day of Jesus Christ;*

## Declarations:
Father in Jesus' name, I decree and declare on today by the Blood of Jesus, whatever You have begun in me You will complete; every dream and vision shall come to pass. Everything that has been dormant shall come to pass. I decree and declare divine breakthrough shall spring forth and favor shall overtake me, In Jesus' name, Amen.

# *Day 8*

It's time for the New!

You have turned the corner into the second half of your spiritual recharge fast. As you have entered into day 8, the number eight represents new beginnings. Beloved, God is preparing something new for you! A new wave is coming! Are you ready? Are you prepared? Do you believe that it's going to happen for you?

Today's scripture says in Isaiah 43:16-19

> *16This is what the LORD says—he who made a way through the sea, a path through the mighty waters,*
>
> *17 who drew out the chariots and horses, the army and reinforcements together, and they lay there, never to rise again, extinguished, snuffed out like a wick:*
>
> *18 "Forget the former things; do not dwell on the past.*
>
> *19 See, I am doing a new thing! Now it springs up; do you not perceive it? I am making a way in the wilderness and streams in the wasteland.*

This section pictures a new exodus for people once again oppressed, as the Israelites had been as slaves in Egypt before the exodus. They would cry to God, and again He would hear and deliver them. A new exodus would take place through a new wilderness. The past miracles were nothing compared to what God would do in the future. God is reminding you that whatever you are facing, never forget that God can and will deliver you. He is the same God that destroyed Pharaoh's army and allowed the people of Israel to walk into a new beginning; new miracles. Starting over and doing something new can be uncomfortable; especially when you are used to living, doing, being, acting and thinking in the same way you are accustomed to or familiar with.

Get ready for the shift and release that is about to happen in your life! How do you prepare? How do you get ready? First, you must forget the former things, let them go and stop dwelling on them. Stop wasting time on toxic and old relationships. Stop dwelling on what you lost, people who lied on you, talked about you, who slandered your name. Release on today! God wants to do something new in your life. He wants to give you a new mindset so stop dwelling on the past it keeps you stuck in that state.

Second, acknowledge that coming out means that you must be conscious of the shift that God is doing and trust Him.

Third, you must believe that God has released you from the things of your past and that you have the right to life anew; a new mindset and the blessings that God is releasing to you in faith, obedience, and trust. God has made a way for you.

I challenge you today to allow yourself to receive all that God is getting ready to release in your hands in this new season of your life.

### *Declarations:*
Father in Jesus' name, I decree and declare that on today, I will no longer dwell on the former things in my life. I

surrender, relinquish, cast away and cast every care upon You. I will remember no more of past hurts, losses, disappointment, frustration, and failures in my old life. I decree and declare today that I will spring forth in the new You have for me. I receive the release of new beginnings in my life. In Jesus' name, Amen!

# *Day 9*

You made it to day 9 and God has begun to fine-tune your spiritual antennas. God's living presence is our greatest joy. His radiant presence helps us grow in strength, grace, and glory.

Beloved, you may be weighed down with the cares of the world and maybe longing to get away from it but you have to desire to meet God inside His dwelling place, His holy temple. You need to know and understand you can meet God anywhere, at any time. You can find joy and strength not only in prayer, music, lessons, and sermons but also in fellowshipping with other believers.

Psalms 84:11 says,

> *[11]For the LORD God is a sun and shield; the LORD bestows favor and honor; no good thing does he withhold from those whose walk is blameless.*

God does not promise to give us everything we think is good, but he will not withhold what is permanently good. He will give us the means to obtain joy, love, and peace. He will give us the means to walk along His paths. We must continue to walk with Him. He will not withhold anything back that will help us serve Him.

### *Declaration:*
Father in Jesus' name, I decree and declare that whatever cares, worries or concerns I may have, I cast them on You. I decree and declare that every hindrance and distraction that is keeping me from experiencing Your presence, by

the Power of the Holy Spirit, I send it back into the lake of fire. Holy Spirit cut off every root of darkness. I desire to experience Your fullness, Your glory, and Your holiness. Your Word declares that You will not withhold any good thing from me. So, Master, I am asking for a full encounter with you. In Jesus' name, Amen!

# *Day 10*

You have made it to day 10. Pray you are beginning to see things clearer, and able to discern things that you once ignored or just didn't see like never before.

This is a very sensitive time for your spiritual growth and deliverance. The enemy is throwing every trick and trap at you to slow down your progress. Do not allow distractions to deter you; it is part of the journey, the process. It is the enemy's job to try to distract you! Remember his job is to kill, steal, and destroy. He is out to destroy you, your purpose and destiny. What the enemy does not know is that you are sold out for your new life and nothing will stop you!

Things will start to happen to you if they haven't already. You will begin to see things more clearly in your dreams.

I challenge you today by your prayers to shut down every negative thought of attacks by the enemy and stand firm in knowing that you are covered by the Blood of Jesus Christ.

Matthew 10:26 says,

> *26" So do not be afraid of them, for there is nothing concealed that will not be disclosed, or hidden that will not be made known.*

## *Declaration:*

Father in Jesus' name, I decree and declare, by the power of the Holy Ghost, that every demonic trip and trap that the enemy has set up against me or my family, may God arise and my enemies be scattered. In Jesus' name, Amen!

# *Day 11*

Thank God for day 11 of the spiritual recharge fast.

The number 11 represents judgment, chaos, and lack of order. The one thing that you cannot allow the enemy to do is to make you think you are naïve. In fact, you've had at least one day during the spiritual recharge fast where things went crazy and the distractions almost took you off course.

The enemy finds time to use situations to hit you with doubt, fear, anxiety, guilt, and shame. Thank God you are mature enough to pick up where the enemy tried to take you off course.

2 Corinthian 2:9-11 says,

> *9Another reason I wrote you was to see if you would stand the test and be obedient in everything.*
>
> *10Anyone you forgive, I also forgive. And what I have forgiven—if there was anything to forgive—I have forgiven in the sight of Christ for your sake,*
>
> *11 in order that Satan might not outwit us. For we are not unaware of his schemes.*

This scripture is a reminder that we must always be watchful of how Satan will use circumstances, situations, and people to undermine you.

I challenge you today to be still, pray and let go of whatever has you caught in; a place of fear, anger or offense. You are stronger than you think you are! Do not let the enemy get you caught up in his traps. This is your time of release; release from past hurts, offense, financial chaos, sickness, worry, fear, strongholds, soul- ties, toxic relationships and whatever else has you bound.

You will know when you are released when the things that you thought you could not walk away from become null and void. They no longer have a stronghold over you and your thoughts; it no longer upsets, frustrates or offends you. You will be able to look back at your past hurts and have a present gratitude that it's over.

**Declaration:**
Father in Jesus' name, I decree and declare by the supreme authority that you have given me and authority of the Almighty God, that I will not be overtaken by deceptive devices and schemes of the enemy. In Jesus' name, Amen!

# *Day 12*

Its day 12 of the spiritual recharge and you are in the home stretch. I pray that this fast has been a blessing to you.

One day I was in worship and had a vision of me underwater trying to swim to the top, but I could not because bricks of cement were wrapped around my ankles. I could see myself underwater breathing with bubbles coming out of my mouth and nose. I was awake, not drowning or gasping for air. I could hear in my mind calling on God asking Him to help me, save me.

Then, I remembered Isaiah 43:2 says,

> *2When you pass through the waters, I will be with you; and when you pass through the rivers, they will not sweep over you.*
> *When you walk through the fire, you will not be burned, the flames will not set you ablaze.*

Going through rivers of difficulty will either cause you to drown or force you to grow stronger. If you go in your own strength, you are more likely to drown. If you invite the Lord to go with you, He will protect you.

Psalms 86:7 says:

> *7When I am in distress, I call to you, because you answer me.*

Sometimes our troubles or pain is so great that all we can do is cry out to God. Preserve my life or Save Your servant (Psalm 86:2). And often, when there is no relief in sight, all we do is acknowledge the greatness of God and wait for better days ahead. The conviction that God answers prayer will sustain us in difficult times.

My vision reminded me that despite my circumstances, situations and how this season of my life, was so overwhelming, difficult and challenging that God was with me. Beloved, I want to encourage you on this 12th day, no matter how difficult times may be that in the day of trouble God will answer you.

### *Declaration:*

Father in Jesus' name, I decree and declare on this day, no matter how hard or difficult times are, I will call upon You because I know You will answer me. I decree and declare that my hurt, pain, life struggles, financial drought, mental anguish, depression or oppression will not overtake me. You said, if I go through the waters, you will be with me, fire will not scorch me nor will the rivers overtake me. I come against every demonic spirit that is trying to overtake my mind, peace, joy, and strength. I decree and declare that no devil in hell will have power over me! You have given me power and authority over demons, serpents, and scorpions. So by the power and authority of the Holy Ghost, I override, overtake, overrule, consume and set fire to every plan and scheme and the devices of the enemy. I decree and declare that I will walk in victory. In Jesus' name, Amen!

# *Day 13*

Here you are at day 13. Glory to God Beloved! God has kept His hands on you. As you reflect on these intimate days with God, it is so important that, beyond this fast, you continue to stay on the wall and focus on living a healthy spiritual life. It is important to stay focused on God and the purpose He has for your life.

We are reminded in Nehemiah 4:6-15 to stay on the wall. You have to make up in your mind and your heart that you will keep building, moving and doing what God has called you to do.

Nehemiah 4:6-14 says:

> *6 So we rebuilt the wall till all of it reached half its height, for the people worked with all their heart.*
>
> *7 But when Sanballat, Tobiah, the Arabs, the Ammonites and the people of Ashdod heard that the repairs to Jerusalem's walls had gone ahead and that the gaps were being closed, they were very angry.*
>
> *8 They all plotted together to come and fight against Jerusalem and stir up trouble against it.*
>
> *9 But we prayed to our God and posted a guard day and night to meet this threat.*
>
> *10 Meanwhile, the people in Judah said, "The strength of the laborers is giving out, and there is so much rubble that we cannot rebuild the wall."*

*11 Also our enemies said, "Before they know it or see us, we will be right there among them and will kill them and put an end to the work."*

*12 Then the Jews who lived near them came and told us ten times over, "Wherever you turn, they will attack us."*

*13 Therefore I stationed some of the people behind the lowest points of the wall at the exposed places, posting them by families, with their swords, spears and bows.*

*14 After I looked things over, I stood up and said to the nobles, the officials and the rest of the people, "Don't be afraid of them. Remember the Lord, who is great and awesome, and fight for your families, your sons and your daughters, your wives and your homes."*

The work of rebuilding the wall progressed well because the people had set their hearts and minds on accomplishing the task. They did not lose faith or give up, but they persevered in the work.

If God has called you to a task you must be determined to complete that particular task, even if you face opposition or discouragement. The rewards of work well done will be worth the effort.

Accomplishing any large task is tiring. There are always pressures that foster discouragement; the task seems impossible, we often tell ourselves, beloved, that it can never be finished. The only thing that removes fatigue and discouragement is focusing on God's purpose. Nehemiah reminded the workers of their calling, their goal and God's protection. If you are overwhelmed by an assignment, tired and discouraged, remember God's purpose for your life and His special purpose for you.

Many factors may be working against you right now, it can be your finances, resources, health, or job but stay on the wall, keep praying, planning and preparing.

### *Declaration:*
Father in Jesus' name, I decree and declare that no matter what assignment you have called me to, I will not grow weary in well-doing. I know I will reap the harvest if I faint not. I decree and declare that when the enemy rushes in like a flood, God will raise a standard against my doubt, adversaries, worry, fatigue, and discouragement. God help me to stay focused on my purpose and destiny, In Jesus' name, Amen!

# *Day 14*

You made it to day 14, we give God glory! The number 14 has great significance to it because it implies a double measure of spiritual perfection and represents deliverance or salvation.

Beloved, God has given you another chance to get it right. Another opportunity to walk into a measure of double; double protection and a double anointing. Your passion has been ignited again and you are on a path of divine intelligence and strength like never before! God is doing a new thing in you, and you will see your energy return, as well your zeal for the things of God.

Continue to stay in the presence of God and the Word of God. Tell your past that "YOU WILL NO LONGER DICTATE MY FUTURE!" Claim your victory and take authority over it.

Joel 2:23-27 says,

> *23Be glad, people of Zion, rejoice in the LORD your God, for he has given you the autumn rains because he is faithful. He sends you abundant showers, both autumn and spring rains, as before.*

> *24 The threshing floors will be filled with grain; the vats will overflow with new wine and oil.*

> *25 "I will repay you for the years the locusts have eaten—the great locust and the young locust, the other locusts and the locust swarm---my great army that I sent among you.*

*26 You will have plenty to eat, until you are full, and you will praise the name of the LORD your God, who has worked wonders for you; never again will my people be shamed.*

*27Then you will know that I am in Israel, that I am the LORD your God, and that there is no other; never again will my people be shamed.*

### *Declaration:*

Father in Jesus' name, I decree and declare by the power of the Holy Spirit, whatever the locust worm has eaten will be restored. I decree and declare that my finances, health, and family will be restored. I decree and declare that I am healed, restored and renewed in Jesus' name, Amen!

www.ingramcontent.com/pod-product-compliance
Lightning Source LLC
Chambersburg PA
CBHW071116090426
42737CB00013B/2597